Summary

The legislative branch appropriations bill provides funding for the Senate; House of Representatives; Joint Items; Capitol Police; Office of Compliance; Congressional Budget Office; Architect of the Capitol; Library of Congress, including the Congressional Research Service; Government Printing Office; Government Accountability Office; and Open World Leadership Center.

The legislative branch FY2013 budget request of $4.512 billion, which is submitted to the President by the legislative branch agencies and entities and included in the budget without change, was submitted to Congress on February 13, 2012. The request represents an increase of $205.5 million over the $4.307 billion in discretionary funding provided in Division G of the FY2012 Consolidated Appropriations Act (H.R. 2055, P.L. 112-74), which was enacted on December 23, 2011.

The Subcommittees on the Legislative Branch of the House and Senate Appropriations Committees both held hearings during which Members considered the FY2013 legislative branch requests. Among issues that were considered during hearings were the following:

- the tight budget environment, prioritization of budget resources, and further options for potential savings or efficiencies;

- state and district office security;

- preparations and funding for the January 2013 Presidential Inauguration;

- deferred maintenance around the Capitol Complex; and

- the future of government printing in the digital age.

On May 18, 2012, the House legislative branch subcommittee met to mark up a bill that would provide nearly $3.333 billion for FY2013, a decrease of 1.0% from FY2012 (not including Senate items, which are determined by the Senate). The full committee held its markup on May 31, during which four amendments were considered, and two were adopted. The bill, H.R. 5882, was reported by voice vote.

The legislative branch budget has decreased the last two fiscal years. The FY2012 level represented a decrease of $236.9 million (-5.2%) from the FY2011 level, which represented a $125.1 million decrease (-2.7%) from FY2010. P.L. 112-10 (enacted on April 15, 2011) provided $4.543 billion for FY2011 legislative branch operations. P.L. 111-68 (enacted on October 1, 2009) provided $4.656 billion for FY2010. The FY2010 Supplemental Appropriations Act (P.L. 111-212) provided an additional $12.96 million for the Capitol Police. The FY2009 Omnibus Appropriations Act (P.L. 111-8, enacted on March 11, 2009) provided $4.402 billion. In FY2009, the American Recovery and Reinvestment Act of 2009 (P.L. 111-5) provided an additional $25.0 million for the Government Accountability Office, and the FY2009 Supplemental Appropriations Act (P.L. 111-32) provided $71.6 million for the Capitol Police and $2.0 million for the Congressional Budget Office.

Since FY1976, the legislative branch has represented approximately 0.4% of total discretionary budget authority.

Contents

Figures

Tables

Appendixes

Contacts

Most Recent Developments

The legislative branch budget request of $4.512 billion, which was included in the President's budget, was submitted to Congress on February 13, 2012. The requested level represents a 4.8% ($205.5 million) increase over the FY2012 enacted level.

In February and March 2012, the House and Senate Appropriations Committees' Legislative Branch Subcommittees both held hearings during which Members considered the FY2013 legislative branch requests.

House Appropriations Subcommittee and Full Committee Markups and Report

On May 18, 2012, the House legislative branch subcommittee met to mark up a bill that would provide nearly $3.333 billion for FY2013 (-1.0%), not including Senate items, which are determined by the Senate.

The full committee held its markup on May 31. Among the issues raised at the markup or in the report were district office security, plans to fund the Architect of the Capitol dome project in future years, report language regarding bulk data downloads, and the use of House funds for legal services related to the Defense of Marriage Act.

Four amendments were considered, and two were adopted:

1. A manager's amendment increasing the appropriation for the Botanic Garden by $140,000 and reducing the Government Printing Office revolving fund by the same amount. The amendment, which was adopted, also allows for activities in Union Square that were permissible prior to the transfer of that land to the Architect of the Capitol from the National Park Service (section 212 of the bill).

2. An amendment, offered by Mr. Honda, requiring the House Inspector General to provide the House Appropriations Committee with a copy of each audit and report the office produces (section 104 of the bill). The amendment was adopted.

3. An amendment, offered by Mr. Flake, related to the use of official funds for online advertising, which was not adopted.

4. An amendment, offered by Mr. Flake, requiring each piece of mass mail to include the aggregate cost of the mailing, which was not adopted.

The bill, H.R. 5882 (H.Rept. 112-511), was reported by voice vote.

House Rules Committee

The House Rules Committee announced in a "Dear Colleague" letter issued on June 1, 2012, that Members wishing to offer an amendment to H.R. 5882 must submit copies of the amendment and an explanation by 4 p.m. on June 5. The committee announced a meeting at 3 p.m. on June 6 to consider H.R. 5882.

Prior Year Funding

Division G of the FY2012 Consolidated Appropriations Act (H.R. 2055, P.L. 112-74), which was enacted on December 23, 2011, provided $4.307 billion in discretionary funding for the legislative branch. This level was $236.9 million (5.2%) below the FY2011 enacted level. The legislative branch represents approximately 0.4% of the total discretionary appropriations provided in this act.

Previously, P.L. 112-10 provided $4.543 billion for legislative branch operations in FY2011. This level represented a $125.1 million decrease from the $4.668 billion provided in the FY2010 Legislative Branch Appropriations Act (P.L. 111-68) and the FY2010 Supplemental Appropriations Act (P.L. 111-212). The FY2009 Omnibus Appropriations Act provided $4.402 billion.[1] In FY2009, an additional $25.0 million was provided for the Government Accountability Office (GAO) in the American Recovery and Reinvestment Act of 2009.[2] P.L. 111-32, the FY2009 Supplemental Appropriations Act, also contained funding for the police radio system ($71.6 million) and Congressional Budget Office ($2.0 million).[3]

Figure 1 compares legislative branch discretionary budget authority to total discretionary budget authority since FY1976. It shows the average annual proportion of total discretionary budget authority over this period is 0.4%. The highest proportional full-year level, 0.48%, was in FY1995, and the lowest, 0.31%, was in FY2009.

Table 1 provides additional information on legislative branch funding provided in annual and supplemental appropriations acts.

---

[1] **Table 4** presents information on the FY2012 appropriation and FY2013 budget request for the legislative branch.

[2] P.L. 111-5, February 17, 2009, 123 Stat. 191.

[3] U.S. Congress, conference committee, *Making Supplemental Appropriations for the Fiscal Year Ending September 30, 2009, and for Other Purposes*, report to accompany H.R. 2346, 111th Cong., 1st sess., H.Rept. 111-151 (Washington: GPO, 2009), p. 117.

Figure 1. Legislative Branch as a Proportion of Total Discretionary Budget Authority

Percentage by Fiscal Year, FY1976-FY2012

1.00%
0.90
0.80
0.70
0.60
0.50
0.40
0.30
0.20
0.10
0.00
FY76
FY79
FY82
FY85
FY88
FY91
FY94
FY97
FY00
FY03
FY06
FY09
FY12

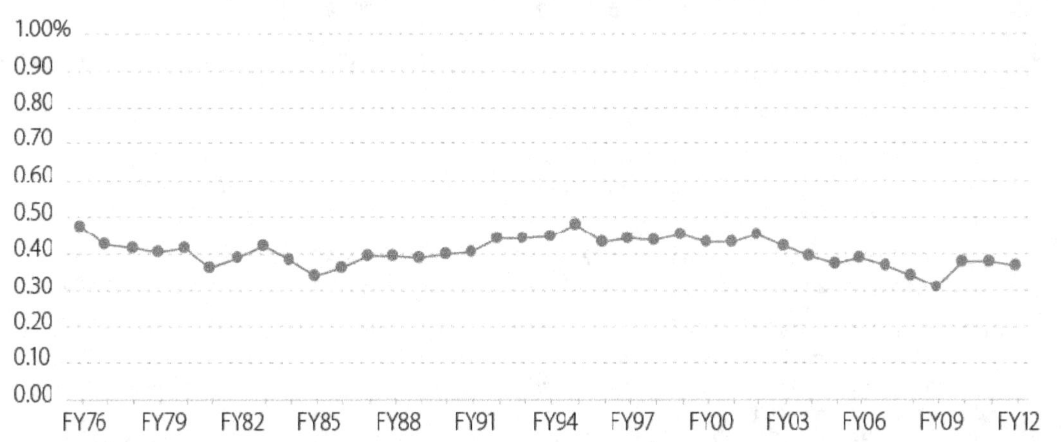

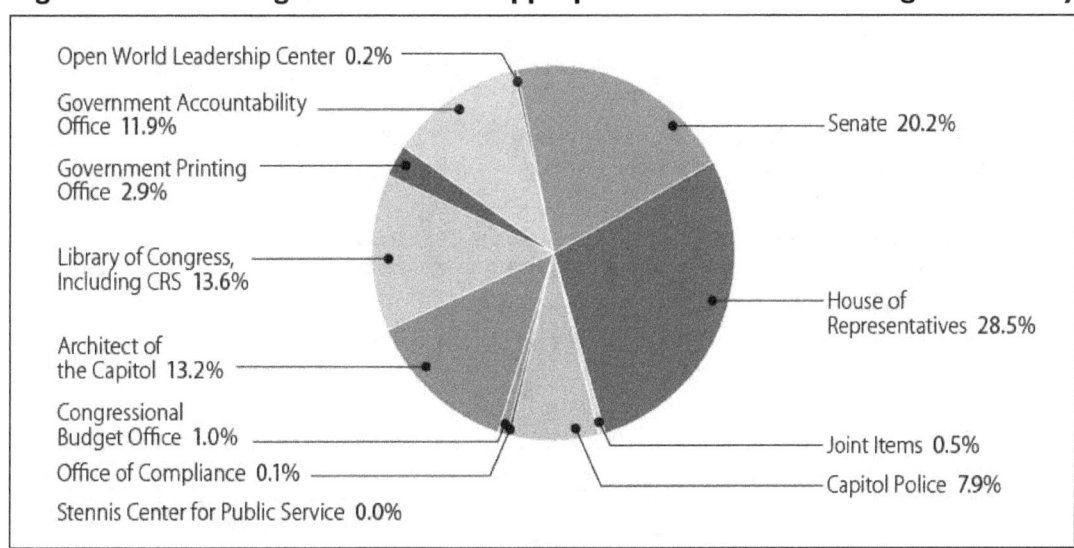

Source: Calculations by CRS with data from Office of Management and Budget (OMB), Historical Tables, *Budget of the United States Government, FY2013, Table 5.4—Discretionary Budget Authority By Agency: 1976–2017*; available at http://www.whitehouse.gov/omb/budget/Historicals.

Notes: This graph does not include the FY1976 transition quarter, so all intervals represent 12 months. FY2012 is derived from the OMB "2012 Estimate." The table has some limitations, since the OMB data do not completely align with items funded in the annual and supplemental legislative branch appropriations acts. The differences may be partially traced to the definition of "legislative branch" in the OMB Public Budget Database "user's guide." Some entities regularly included with the legislative branch in many OMB budget documents, like the United States Tax Court and some Legislative Branch Boards and Commissions, are not funded through the annual legislative branch appropriations acts. Consequently, an examination of the discretionary budget authority listed in the *Historical Tables* reveals some differences with the reported total budget authority provided in the annual legislative branch appropriations acts. The difference in legislative branch budget authority resulting from the different definitions of the legislative branch in the OMB budget documents and in the appropriations acts, however, does not represent a large difference in the proportion of total discretionary budget authority.

Figure 2. FY2012 Legislative Branch Appropriations: Division of Budget Authority

Open World Leadership Center 0.2%
Government Accountability Office 11.9%
Government Printing Office 2.9%
Library of Congress, Including CRS 13.6%
Architect of the Capitol 13.2%
Congressional Budget Office 1.0%
Office of Compliance 0.1%
Stennis Center for Public Service 0.0%
Senate 20.2%
House of Representatives 28.5%
Joint Items 0.5%
Capitol Police 7.9%

Source: P.L. 112-74, calculations by the Congressional Research Service.

Notes: Does not include offsetting collections or authority to spend receipts. Numbers may not add due to rounding.

Table 1. Legislative Branch Appropriations, FY2000-FY2012

(budget authority in billions of dollars)

2000	2001	2002	2003	2004	2005	2006	2007	2008	2009	2010	2011	2012
2.486[a]	2.730[b]	3.252[c]	3.461[d]	3.528[e]	3.640[f]	3.793[g]	3.852[h]	3.970	4.501[i]	4.669[j]	4.543[k]	4.307

Source: Congressional Research Service.

Notes: These figures represent current dollars, exclude permanent budget authorities, and contain supplementals and rescissions. Permanent budget authorities, including funding for Member pay, are not included in the annual legislative branch appropriations bill but are automatically funded each year.

a. Includes budget authority contained in the FY2000 Legislative Branch Appropriations Act (P.L. 106-57), a supplemental and a 0.38% rescission in P.L. 106-113, and supplementals in P.L. 106-246 and P.L. 106-554.

b. This figure contains (1) FY2001 appropriations contained in H.R. 5657, legislative branch appropriations bill; (2) FY2001 supplemental appropriations of $118.0 million and a 0.22% across-the-board rescission contained in H.R. 5666, miscellaneous appropriations bill; and (3) FY2001 supplemental appropriations of $79.5 million contained in H.R. 2216 (P.L. 107-20). H.R. 5657 and H.R. 5666 were incorporated by reference in P.L. 106-554, FY2001 Consolidated Appropriations Act. The first FY2001 legislative branch appropriations bill, H.R. 4516, was vetoed October 30, 2000. The second legislative branch appropriations bill, H.R. 5657, was introduced December 14, 2000, and incorporated in P.L. 106-554. This figure does not reflect any terrorism supplemental funds released pursuant to P.L. 107-38.

c. This figure contains appropriations in P.L. 107-68, transfers from the legislative branch emergency response fund pursuant to P.L. 107-117, and FY2002 supplemental appropriations in P.L. 107-206.

d. This figure contains appropriations in P.L. 108-7, FY2003 Omnibus Appropriations Act, and supplemental appropriations in P.L. 108-11.

e. This figure contains appropriations in P.L. 108-83, FY2004 Legislative Branch Appropriations Act. Additional FY2004 provisions which did not contain appropriations were contained in P.L. 108-199, the FY2004 Consolidated Appropriations Act.

f. This figure contains appropriations in P.L. 108-447, Consolidated Appropriations Act, FY2005 (adjusted by a 0.80% rescission also contained in P.L. 108-447), and P.L. 109-13, FY2005 Emergency Supplemental.

g. This figure contains appropriations in P.L. 109-55, FY2006 Legislative Branch Appropriations Act (adjusted by a 1.0% rescission contained in P.L. 109-148), and the FY2006 Emergency Supplemental Appropriations Act (P.L. 109-234).

h. This figure contains appropriations in P.L. 110-5, the Revised Continuing Appropriations Resolution, 2007, and P.L. 110-28, the U.S. Troop Readiness, Veterans' Care, Katrina Recovery, and Iraq Accountability Appropriations Act, 2007.

i. This figure contains the appropriations in P.L. 110-161, the FY2009 Omnibus Appropriations Act, $25.0 million for the legislative branch contained in the American Recovery and Reinvestment Act of 2009 (P.L. 111-5), and $73.6 million contained in P.L. 111-32.

j. This figure contains the appropriations in P.L. 111-68, the FY2010 Legislative Branch Appropriations Act, and the $12.96 million in supplemental appropriations provided for the U.S. Capitol Police in P.L. 111-212.

k. This figure does not include scorekeeping adjustment.

Status of FY2013 Appropriations

Table 2. Status of Legislative Branch Appropriations, FY2013

Committee Markup		House Report	House Passage	Senate Report	Senate Passage	Conference Report	Conference Report Approval		Public Law
House	Senate						House	Senate	
5/31/12		H.Rept. 112-511 (H.R. 5882)							

Source: Congressional Research Service.

Note: In recent years, the House has had a subcommittee markup, while the Senate has held a markup for the legislative branch only at the full committee level.

Action on the FY2013 Legislative Branch Appropriations Bill

Submission of FY2013 Budget Request on February 13, 2012

The *FY2013 U.S. Budget* submitted on February 13, 2012, contained a request for $4.512 billion in new budget authority for legislative branch activities, an increase of approximately 4.8% from the FY2012 enacted level.[4]

By law, the legislative branch request is submitted to the President and included in the budget without change.[5]

Senate and House Hearings on the FY2013 Budget Requests

Table 3 lists the dates of hearings of the Legislative Branch Subcommittees in 2012.

Table 3. Dates of House and Senate Hearings on Legislative Branch Requests

	House of Representatives	Senate
Senate	—	March 22, 2012
House of Representatives	March 27, 2012	—
Capitol Police	February 8, 2012	March 22, 2012

[4] Office of Management and Budget, *Analytical Perspectives, Budget of the United States Government, FY2013*, Table 33-1, "Federal Programs by Agency and Account" (Washington: GPO, 2012), pp. 2-16; and Office of Management and Budget, *Appendix, Budget of the United States Government, FY2013* (Washington: GPO, 2012), pp. 17-49.

[5] Pursuant to 31 U.S.C. 1105, "Estimated expenditures and proposed appropriations for the legislative branch and the judicial branch to be included in each budget ... shall be submitted to the President ... and included in the budget by the President without change." Division C of the FY2012 Consolidated Appropriations Act (P.L. 112-74) added language to 31 U.S.C. 1107 relating to budget amendments, stating: "The President shall transmit promptly to Congress without change, proposed deficiency and supplemental appropriations submitted to the President by the legislative branch and the judicial branch."

	House of Representatives	Senate
Office of Compliance	—	March 1, 2012
Congressional Budget Office	February 7, 2012	March 15, 2012
Architect of the Capitol	February 9, 2012	March 1, 2012
Library of Congress, including the Congressional Research Service	February 7, 2012	March 1, 2012
Government Printing Office	February 7, 2012	March 15, 2012
Government Accountability Office	February 7, 2012	March 15, 2012
Open World Leadership Center	—	March 1, 2012
Members/Public Witnesses	—a	—

Source: Congressional Research Service.

Note:

a. The House subcommittee announced that it would be accepting testimony for the record from Members and outside witnesses through March 20, 2012.

The Budget Control Act (BCA) and FY2013 Spending Levels

FY2013 discretionary appropriations will be considered in the context of the Budget Control Act of 2011 (BCA, P.L. 112-25), which established discretionary spending limits for FY2012 to FY2021. The BCA also tasked a Joint Select Committee on Deficit Reduction to develop a federal deficit reduction plan for Congress and the President to enact by January 15, 2012. The failure of Congress and the President to enact deficit reduction legislation by that date triggered an automatic spending reduction process established by the BCA, consisting of a combination of sequestration and lower discretionary spending caps, to begin on January 2, 2013. The sequestration process for FY2013 requires across-the-board spending cuts at the account and program level to achieve equal budget reductions from both defense and nondefense funding at a percentage to be announced by the Office of Management and Budget. As a result, the FY2013 legislative branch appropriation will be considered by Congress with the understanding that enacted funding levels will likely be subject to significant cuts in the nondefense category under the sequestration process unless legislation specifically repealing the sequestration provisions of the BCA is enacted by Congress before next January.

Additionally, the House has passed a budget resolution at a level below the spending cap contained in the BCA, providing $1.028 trillion in overall discretionary budget authority (H.Con.Res. 112).

The Senate Appropriations Committee also adopted, on April 19, 2012, 302(b) budget allocations, allocating $4.42 billion in discretionary spending for the legislative branch (S.Rept. 112-156).

FY2013 Legislative Branch Funding Issues

The following sections discuss the various legislative branch accounts as well as issues discussed during the hearings on the budget requests.

Senate[6]

Overall Funding

The Senate requested $910.5 million for FY2013, an increase of 4.8% ($41.9 million) over the FY2012 level of $868.6 million.

The FY2012 level represented a decrease of $45.6 million (-5.0%) from the $914.2 million provided in FY2011, and the FY2011 level represented a reduction of $12.0 million (-1.3%) from the FY2010 level of $926.2 million.

FY2013 requests and FY2012 funding levels for headings within the Senate account are presented in **Table 5**.

Senate Committee Funding

Appropriations for Senate committees are contained in two accounts:[7]

- The *inquiries and investigations account* contains funds for all Senate committees except Appropriations. The Senate requested $138.0 million for inquiries and investigations, an increase of $6.7 million (5.1%) from the $131.3 million provided in FY2012. The FY2012 level was a decrease of $8.9 million (-6.4%) from the $140.2 million provided in FY2011 and FY2010.

- The *Committee on Appropriations account* contains funds for the Senate Appropriations Committee. The Senate requested $14.9 million, which is equal to the FY2012 level.

Senators' Official Personnel and Office Expense Account

The Senators' Official Personnel and Office Expense Account provides each Senator with funds to administer an office. It consists of an administrative and clerical assistance allowance, a legislative assistance allowance, and an official office expense allowance. The funds may be used for any category of expenses, subject to limitations on official mail.

The Senate requested $425.6 million for FY2013, an increase of $29.4 million (7.4%) from the FY2012 level of $396.2 million. The FY2012 level represented a decrease of $13.0 million (-3.2%) from the FY2011 level of $409.2 million. The FY2012 decrease followed a decrease in FY2011 of $12.8 million (-3.0%) from the FY2010 level of $422.0 million.[8]

---

[6] In keeping with tradition, H.R. 5882, as reported by the House Appropriations Committee, does not include Senate items.

[7] For additional information on committee funding, see CRS Report R40424, *Senate Committee Expenditures Resolutions, 112th Congress, and Funding Authorizations Since 1995*, by Matthew Eric Glassman.

[8] The FY2011 act (P.L. 112-10) also contained language stating, "each Senator's official personnel and office expense allowance (including the allowance for administrative and clerical assistance, the salaries allowance for legislative assistance to Senators, as authorized by the Legislative Branch Appropriation Act, 1978 (P.L. 95-94), and the office expense allowance for each Senator's office for each State) in effect immediately before the date of enactment of this section shall be reduced by 5 percent."

Highlights of the Senate Hearing on the FY2013 Budget of the Senate

At a hearing on March 22, 2012, the Senate subcommittee discussed new responsibilities for the Secretary of the Senate and the Sergeant at Arms related to financial disclosure forms required under the STOCK Act (S. 2038, P.L. 112-105);[9] the Senate Information Services Program (SIS) operating budget; requested increases for state office security; and costs related to the January 2013 Presidential Inauguration.

House of Representatives

Overall Funding

H.R. 5882, as reported by the House Appropriations Committee, provides $1.226 billion for FY2013, the same level as requested for FY2013 and provided in FY2012.

The FY2012 level represented a decrease of $85.7 million (-6.5%) from the FY2011 level of $1.311 billion. The FY2011 level represented a decrease of $57.6 million (-4.2%) from the FY2010 level of $1.369 billion.

In related action, on January 6, 2011, the House agreed to H.Res. 22 (112th Congress), which reduced the authorized amounts for the Members' Representational Allowances, House leadership offices, and all committees except the Committee on Appropriations by 5%, with a 9% reduction for the Committee on Appropriations.

FY2013 requests and FY2012 funding levels for headings in the House of Representatives account are presented in **Table 6**.

House Committee Funding[10]

Funding for House committees is contained in the appropriation heading "committee employees," which comprises two subheadings.

The first subheading contains funds for personnel and nonpersonnel expenses of House committees, except the Appropriations Committee, as authorized by the House in a committee expense resolution. H.R. 5882, as reported, would provide the FY2012 level of $126.0 million. The House had requested $126.4 million, an increase of $399,000 (0.3%). The FY2012 level was a decrease of $8.6 million from the $134.5 million provided for FY2011. The FY2011 level was a decrease of $5.3 million from the $139.9 million provided in FY2010.

---

[9] The Congressional Budget Office cost estimate of this legislation, issued January 31, 2012, is available at http://cbo.gov/sites/default/files/cbofiles/attachments/s2038.pdf. It states: "Based on information from Congressional staff, CBO estimates that implementing the financial disclosure system required under S. 2038 would cost $4 million over the 2012-2013 period primarily for new computer hardware and software and additional labor. In addition, maintaining the new system would cost $1 million annually, CBO estimates."

[10] For additional information on committee funding, CRS Report RL32794, *House Committee Funding Requests and Authorizations, 104th-112th Congresses*, by Matthew Eric Glassman.

The second subheading contains funds for the personnel and nonpersonnel expenses of the Committee on Appropriations. H.R. 5882, as reported, would provide $26.7 million for FY2013, the same level as the FY2013 request and the FY2012 enacted level. The FY2012 level was a decrease of $1.8 million from the FY2011 level of $28.5 million, which was a decrease of $2.8 million from the FY2010 level of $31.3 million.

Members' Representational Allowance[11]

The Members' Representational Allowance (MRA) is available to support Members in their official and representational duties. The House-reported bill would provide $573.9 million, the same level as provided for FY2012 and contained in the FY2013 request. This level was $39.1 million less than the $613.1 million provided in FY2011. The FY2011 level was a decrease of nearly $47.0 million from the $660.0 million provided in FY2010.

Highlights of the House Hearing on the FY2013 Budget of the House of Representatives

At a hearing on March 27, 2012, the House subcommittee continued discussion from the FY2012 hearings related to district office security and expenses for legal services related to the Defense of Marriage Act, as well as reduced budgets for Member offices; subscription services; implementation of the STOCK Act, including costs related to new public filing and disclosure responsibilities of the Clerk of the House; diversity policies; constitutional authority statements required pursuant to House Rule XII and H.Res. 5; and the activities of the House Inspector General.

Support Agency Funding

U.S. Capitol Police

The U.S. Capitol Police (USCP) are responsible for the security of the Capitol Complex including the U.S. Capitol, the House and Senate office buildings, the U.S. Botanic Garden, and the Library of Congress buildings and adjacent grounds.

The USCP requested $373.8 million for FY2013, an increase of $33.6 million (9.9%). The House-reported version of H.R. 5882 would provide $360.1 million, an increase of $20.0 million (5.9%). The FY2012 Consolidated Appropriations Act provided $340.1 million, the same level as for FY2011. Previously, the FY2010 appropriations act provided $328.3 million, and P.L. 111-212 provided an additional $12.96 million in supplemental appropriations.

The USCP FY2013 request and FY2012 funding level are presented in **Table 7**.

Appropriations for the police are contained in two accounts—a *salaries account* and a *general expenses account*. The salaries account contains funds for the salaries of employees; overtime pay; hazardous duty pay differential; and government contributions for employee health,

---

[11] For additional information, see CRS Report R40962, *Members' Representational Allowance: History and Usage*, by Ida A. Brudnick.

retirement, Social Security, professional liability insurance, and other benefit programs. The general expenses account contains funds for expenses of vehicles; communications equipment; security equipment and its installation; dignitary protection; intelligence analysis; hazardous material response; uniforms; weapons; training programs; medical, forensic, and communications services; travel; relocation of instructors for the Federal Law Enforcement Training Center; and other administrative and technical support, among other expenses. The House-reported bill would provide $297.1 million for salaries (an increase of nearly $20.0 million, or 7.2%) and $63.0 million for expenses (the same as provided in FY2012). The Capitol Police requested $303.1 million for salaries (an increase of nearly $26 million, or 9.4%) and $70.6 million (an increase of $7.6 million, or 12.1%). The FY2012 Consolidated Appropriations Act provided the same level as in FY2011 for both salaries and general expenses.

Another appropriation relating to the Capitol Police appears within the Architect of the Capitol account for Capitol Police buildings and grounds. The House-reported bill would provide $20.9 million (a decrease of $633,000, or -2.9%) from the FY2012 level of $21.5 million. The Capitol Police had requested $30.8 million, an increase of $9.3 million (43.3%). The FY2011 enacted level was nearly $27.0 million.

Administrative Provisions

The House-reported bill includes two administrative provisions, providing authority to transfer between salaries and expenses (section 1001) and making "available balances of expired United States Capitol Police appropriations" available for "deposit to the credit of the Employees' Compensation Fund required by section 8147(b) of title 5, United States Code" (section 1002).

Highlights of the House and Senate Hearings on the FY2013 Budget of the U.S. Capitol Police

At a hearing on March 22, 2012, the Senate subcommittee discussed costs related to the January 2013 Presidential Inauguration; overtime costs; and the radio modernization project.

On February 8, 2012, the House subcommittee discussed the response to the earthquake on August 23, 2011; the transfer of Union Square and public access; the status of a discrimination lawsuit; the mission of the Capitol Police; measures to control overtime costs; inauguration planning; and district office security.

Architect of the Capitol

The Architect of the Capitol (AOC) is responsible for the maintenance, operation, development, and preservation of the United States Capitol Complex, which includes the Capitol and its grounds, House and Senate office buildings, Library of Congress buildings and grounds, Capitol power plant, Botanic Garden, Capitol Visitor Center, and Capitol Police buildings and grounds. The Architect is responsible for the Supreme Court buildings and grounds, but appropriations for their expenses are not contained in the legislative branch appropriations bill.

Overall Funding Levels

Operations of the Architect are funded in the following 10 accounts: general administration, Capitol building, Capitol grounds, Senate office buildings, House office buildings, Capitol power plant, Library buildings and grounds, Capitol Police buildings and grounds, Capitol Visitor Center, and Botanic Garden.

The Architect requested $668.2 million, an increase of $100.7 million (17.7%) from the FY2012 level of $567.5 million. The House-reported bill would provide $444.0 million, not including Senate items.

The FY2012 level represented a decrease of $32.9 million (-5.5%) from the FY2011 enacted level of $600.4 million (not including a rescission of $14.6 million in unobligated amounts of prior year appropriations for the Capitol Visitor Center contained in the FY2011 act). The FY2011 level represented a decrease of $1.2 million (-0.2%) from the $601.6 million provided in FY2010. In FY2010, a 21.7% increase (or $644.6 million) was requested, and a 13.6% increase was provided ($601.6 million).[12] In FY2009, a 55.4% increase ($642.7 million) was requested, and a 28% increase ($529.6 million) was provided. The FY2008 budget authority ($413.5 million) represented a decrease of 8.1% from the $449.9 million (including supplemental appropriations) provided in FY2007.

The FY2013 request and FY2012 funding level for each of the AOC accounts are presented in **Table 8**.

Administrative Provision

The House-reported bill includes an administrative provision making "available balances of expired Architect of the Capitol appropriations" available for "deposit to the credit of the Employees' Compensation Fund required by section 8147(b) of title 5, United States Code" (section 1301).

Highlights of the House and Senate Hearings on the FY2013 Budget of the Architect of the Capitol

At a hearing on March 1, 2012, the Senate subcommittee discussed the Capitol Dome skirt project; the Capitol power plant and chiller capacity; potential consolidation of financial management systems; fire and life safety priorities; and improvements to Union Square, which includes the Capitol reflecting pool and the Grant Memorial.

At a hearing on February 9, 2012, the House subcommittee discussed the AOC policy on workplace harassment; maintenance of the Capitol Visitor Center; the potential for co-generation at the Capitol power plant; garage maintenance; and the occupation of Federal Office Building #8.

---

[12] Under the Capitol Visitor Center Act of 2008 (P.L. 110-437), funding for the Capitol Guide Service was transferred to the Architect of the Capitol.

Congressional Budget Office (CBO)

CBO is a nonpartisan congressional agency created to provide objective economic and budgetary analysis to Congress. CBO cost estimates are required for any measure reported by a regular or conference committee that may vary revenues or expenditures.[13]

CBO requested $44.6 million for FY2013, an $850,000 increase (1.9%) from the $43.8 million provided for FY2012. The House-reported bill would provide $44.3 million, an increase of $493,000 (1.1%).

The FY2012 level represented a decrease of 6.4% from the FY2011 level of $46.8 million. CBO received $45.2 million for FY2010; $44.1 million was provided in the FY2009 Omnibus Appropriations Act (P.L. 111-8), and $2.0 million, to remain available through FY2010, was provided in the FY2009 Supplemental Appropriations Act (P.L. 111-32).

Administrative Provisions

CBO has requested two administrative provisions for FY2013. The requested provisions would

1. allow CBO's appropriation to be used to pay the compensation of certain employees with non-immigrant visas, a provision also requested in FY2012, and

2. allow CBO to accept the use of voluntary student services as part of an agency program established for the purpose of providing educational experiences for the student.

The House-reported bill contains the voluntary student services provision.

Highlights of the House and Senate Hearings on the FY2013 Budget of CBO

At the House hearing on February 7, 2012, the subcommittee discussed zero-based budgeting; CBO's scorekeeping unit; proposed legislation which would require dynamic scoring; and proposals to move to biennial budgeting.

At a hearing on March 15, 2012, the Senate subcommittee discussed CBO's staffing plan and resources, including deferred IT purchases and upgrades.

Library of Congress (LOC)

The Library of Congress serves simultaneously as Congress's parliamentary library and the de facto national library of the United States. Its broader services to the nation include the acquisition, maintenance, and preservation of a collection of more than 147 million items[14] in a wide range of traditional and new media; service to the general public and scholarly and library

---

[13] The Congressional Budget Office is required to use estimates provided by the Joint Committee on Taxation for all revenue legislation (Balanced Budget and Emergency Deficit Control Act of 1985, P.L. 99-177, §273, 99 Stat.1098, December 12, 1985; 2 U.S.C. §621 (et seq.)).

[14] Figure obtained from the *Annual Report of the Librarian of Congress for Fiscal Year 2010*, Library of Congress, Washington, DC, 2011. Available at http://www.loc.gov/about/reports/.

communities; administration of U.S. copyright laws by its Copyright Office; and administration of a national program to provide reading material to the blind and physically handicapped. Its direct services to Congress include the provision of legal research and law-related services by the Law Library of Congress, and a broad range of activities by the Congressional Research Service (CRS), including in-depth and nonpartisan public policy research, analysis, and legislative assistance for Members and committees and their staff; congressional staff training; information and statistics retrieval; and continuing legal education for Members of both chambers and congressional staff.

The Library requested $603.6 million for FY2013, an increase of $16.2 million (2.8%) from the FY2012 level of $587.3 million. The House-reported bill would provide $592.6 million, an increase of $5.3 million (0.9%).

The FY2012 level represented a decrease of $41.3 million (-6.6%) from the FY2011 level of $628.7 million. The FY2011 level represented a decrease of $14.7 million (-2.3%) from the $643.3 million provided in FY2010. The FY2010 level represented an increase of 6.0% over the FY2009 level of $607.1 million,[15] and the FY2009 level represented an increase of approximately 7.8% over the $563.0 million provided in the FY2008 Consolidated Appropriations Act. These figures do not include additional authority to spend receipts.[16]

The FY2013 budget contains the following headings:

- Salaries and expenses—The House-reported bill would provide $415.7 million (an increase of $1.9 million, or 0.5%). The Library requested $423.7 million (not including $6.35 million in authority to spend receipts), an increase of $9.96 million (2.4%) from the FY2012 level of $413.7 million (not including $6.35 million in authority to spend receipts). The FY2012 level represented a decrease of $18.0 million (-4.2%) from the FY2011 level of $431.8 million. The FY2011 level was an $8.0 million decrease (-1.8%) from the $439.8 million provided for FY2010.

- Copyright Office—The House-reported bill would provide $18.5 million (an increase of $2.4 million, or 14.8%). The Library requested $19.2 million for the copyright office, an increase of $3.0 million (18.7%). The FY2012 Consolidated Appropriations Act provided $16.1 million, a decrease of $1.7 million (-9.5%). The FY2011 level of $17.8 million was a decrease of $3.0 million (-14.6%) from the $20.9 million provided for FY2010. These levels do not include authority to spend receipts.

- Congressional Research Service—The House-reported bill would provide $107.7 million (an increase of $878,000, or 0.8%).[17] The FY2013 request includes $109.2 million for CRS, an increase of $2.4 million (2.3%). The FY2012 Consolidated Appropriations Act provided $106.8 million, a decrease of $4.2

---

[15] This percentage is not adjusted for non-recurring costs, including the transfer of the Library of Congress Police to the Capitol Police.

[16] An example of receipts are fees paid to the LOC for copyright registration.

[17] The House report also notes that the retention of $1.0 million provided in FY2012 for contract services would result in an actual increase of "$1,878,000, over the fiscal year 2012 enacted level" (U.S. Congress, House Committee on Appropriations, *FY2013 Legislative Branch Appropriations Bill*, H.Rept. 112-511, report to accompany H.R. 5882 (Washington: GPO, 2012), p. 16).

million (-3.8%) from the FY2011 level of $111.0 million. The FY2011 level was a decrease of $1.5 million (-1.3%) from the $112.5 million provided for FY2010.

- Books for the Blind and Physically Handicapped—The House-reported bill would provide $50.8 million (an increase of $101,000, or 0.2%). The Library requested $51.5 million, an increase of $848,000 (1.7%). The FY2012 Consolidated Appropriations Act provided $50.7 million, a decrease of $17.4 million (-25.5%) from the $68.0 million provided for FY2011. The FY2011 level was a decrease of $2.1 million (-3.0%) from the $70.2 million provided for FY2010.

The Architect's budget also contains funds for the Library buildings and grounds. The House-reported bill would provide $30.7 million (a decrease of $16.2 million, or -34.6%). The FY2013 request includes $53.6 million (an increase of $6.7 million, or 14.3%). The FY2012 Consolidated Appropriations Act provided $46.9 million, an increase of $1.2 million (2.6%) from the $45.7 million provided for FY2011. The FY2011 level represented a 0.2% reduction (-$92,000) from the $45.8 million provided for Library buildings and grounds in FY2010.

Administrative Provisions

The Library requested two administrative provisions, which were included in the House-reported bill, related to authority to obligate funds for reimbursable and revolving fund activities and providing transfer authority.

Highlights of the House and Senate Hearings on the FY2013 Budget of the Library of Congress

At a hearing on February 7, 2012, the House subcommittee examined zero-based budgeting efforts; inflationary costs; the Library's Twitter archive; General Services Administration (GSA) rental costs; the Veterans' Oral History Project and the Civil Rights Oral History Project; the copyright small claims court project; and the Library's overseas operations, including the operation of the Cairo office during the "Arab Spring."

At a hearing on March 1, 2012, the Senate subcommittee discussed the consequences of budget cuts in FY2011 and FY2012 and prioritization of the budget for FY2013; the buyout conducted in the first quarter of FY2012 and the departure of 186 staff; and the Library's request for the Ft. Meade storage module.

Government Accountability Office (GAO)

GAO works for Congress by responding to requests for studies of federal government programs and expenditures. GAO may also initiate its own work.[18] Formerly the General Accounting Office, the agency was renamed the Government Accountability Office effective July 7, 2004.

---

[18] GAO's guidelines for initiating studies are contained in U.S. Government Accountability Office, *GAO's Congressional Protocols*, GAO-04-310G (Washington: GAO, 2004). Posted on the website of the Government Accountability Office at http://www.gao.gov/special.pubs/d04310g.pdf.

The House-reported bill would provide $519.8 million (an increase of $8.5 million, or 1.7%). GAO requested $526.2 million for FY2013, an increase of $14.9 million (2.9%) over the $511.3 million provided in FY2012. The FY2012 level represented a decrease of $34.96 million (-6.4%) from the $546.3 million provided for FY2011. The FY2011 level was a decrease of $10.6 million (-1.9%) from the $556.9 million GAO received in FY2010. GAO received $531.0 million in the FY2009 Omnibus Appropriations Act and an additional $25.0 million in P.L. 111-5 to cover responsibilities under the American Recovery and Reinvestment Act of 2009. These levels do not include offsetting collections.[19]

Administrative Provision

The House-reported bill includes an administrative provision making "available balances of expired Government Accountability Office appropriations" available for "deposit to the credit of the Employees' Compensation Fund required by section 8147(b) of title 5, United States Code" (section 1501).

Highlights of House and Senate Hearings on the FY2013 Budget of the GAO

At the House hearing on February 7, 2012, the subcommittee discussed issues including zero-based budgeting; prioritization of items in the FY2013 budget request; the buyout program conducted in 2011; the GAO student loan repayment program; prioritization of congressional requests; GAO's reports on high-risk and duplicative programs; diversity; and GAO's training program.

The Senate subcommittee met on March 15, 2012, and discussed GAO's staffing requests; the potential of a consolidation of financial management systems; zero-based budgeting; and costs for audits related to the Troubled Asset Relief Program (TARP).

Government Printing Office (GPO)[20]

The House-reported bill would provide $122.5 million, a decrease of $3.7 million (-3.0%). GPO requested $126.2 million for FY2013, the same level provided in FY2012. This level represents a decrease of $8.9 million (-6.6%) from the $135.1 million provided for FY2011, which was a decrease of $12.4 million (-8.4%) from the $147.5 million for FY2010. The FY2010 level represented an increase of $6.9 million (4.9%) over the $140.6 million provided in the FY2009 Omnibus Appropriations Act. The FY2009 level represented an increase of $15.9 million (12.7%) over the $124.7 million provided in the FY2008 Consolidated Appropriations Act.

GPO's budget authority is contained in three accounts: (1) congressional printing and binding, (2) Office of Superintendent of Documents (salaries and expenses), and (3) the revolving fund.

- Congressional printing and binding—The House-reported bill would provide $83.6 million, a decrease of $7.1 million (-7.8%). GPO requested $83.6 million, a decrease of $7.1 million (-7.8%) from the FY2012 level of $90.7 million. The

---

[19] Offsetting collections include funds derived from reimbursable audits and rental of space in the GAO building.

[20] For additional information on GPO, see CRS Report R40897, *Congressional Printing: Background and Issues for Congress*, by R. Eric Petersen and Amber Hope Wilhelm.

FY2012 level represented a decrease of $2.9 million (-3.1%) from the $93.6 million provided for FY2011. The FY2010 appropriations act provided $93.8 million.

- Office of Superintendent of Documents (salaries and expenses)—The House-reported bill would provide $34.7 million, a decrease of $272,000 (-0.8%). GPO requested $34.7 million, a decrease of $272,000 (-0.8%) from the FY2012 level of $35.0 million. The FY2012 level was a decrease of $4.8 million (-12.1%) from the $39.8 million provided for FY2011. The FY2010 appropriations act provided $40.9 million.

- Revolving fund—The House-reported bill would provide $4.1 million, an increase of $3.6 million. The revolving fund supports the operation and maintenance of the Government Printing Office.[21] GPO requested $7.8 million, an increase of $7.3 million from the FY2012 level of $500,000. Previously, the FY2011 act provided $1.66 million, and the FY2010 act provided $12.8 million for the revolving fund.

The congressional printing and binding account pays for expenses of printing and binding required for congressional use, and for statutorily authorized printing, binding, and distribution of government publications for specified recipients at no charge. Included within these publications are the *Congressional Record*; *Congressional Directory*; Senate and House Journals; memorial addresses of Members; nominations; *U.S. Code* and supplements; serial sets; publications printed without a document or report number, for example, laws and treaties; envelopes provided to Members of Congress for the mailing of documents; House and Senate business and committee calendars; bills, resolutions, and amendments; committee reports and prints; committee hearings; and other documents.

The Office of Superintendent of Documents account funds the mailing of government documents for Members of Congress and federal agencies, as statutorily authorized; the compilation of catalogs and indexes of government publications; and the cataloging, indexing, and distribution of government publications to the Federal Depository and International Exchange libraries, and to other individuals and entities, as authorized by law.

Highlights of House and Senate Hearings on the FY2013 Budget of the Government Printing Office

The House subcommittee met on February 7, 2012, to discuss GPO's FY2013 budget request. Among the items addressed were a survey of congressional offices to determine preferred *Congressional Record* distribution levels, which reduced the number of copies by 400; the use of XML; diversity and training opportunities; and the future of printing in a digital era.

The Senate subcommittee held its FY2013 budget request hearing on March 15, 2012. The subcommittee discussed GPO's experience with zero-based budgeting and its staffing level following the implementation of a buyout program in 2011.

---

[21] For additional information, see CRS Report R40939, *Legislative Branch Revolving Funds*, by Ida A. Brudnick and Jacob R. Straus.

Office of Compliance

The Office of Compliance is an independent and nonpartisan agency within the legislative branch. It was established to administer and enforce the Congressional Accountability Act, which was enacted in 1995.[22] The act applies various employment and workplace safety laws to Congress and certain legislative branch entities.[23]

The House-reported bill would provide $3.8 million, equivalent to the FY2012 enacted level. The Office of Compliance had requested $4.2 million, an increase of $389,000 (10.2%).

The FY2012 level represented a decrease of $260,000 (-6.4%) from the $4.08 million provided in P.L. 112-10 for FY2011. The FY2011 level represented a decrease of $300,000 (-6.9%) from the $4.4 million provided in FY2010. The FY2010 level represented an increase of 7.5% from the $4.1 million provided in the FY2009 Omnibus, which was an increase of 21.8% over the FY2008 level of $3.3 million.

Administrative Provision

The House-reported bill also contains an administrative provision related to awards and settlements under the Congressional Accountability Act.

Highlights of the Senate Hearing on the FY2013 Budget of the Office of Compliance

The Senate held a hearing on the FY2013 budget request on March 1, 2012. The subcommittee discussed consequences of reduced funding, including reduced staff and training, and collaboration with the Architect of the Capitol.

Open World Leadership Center

The Open World Leadership Center administers a program that supports democratic changes in other countries by inviting their leaders to observe democracy and free enterprise in the United States. The first program was authorized by Congress in 1999 to support the relationship between Russia and the United States. The program encouraged young federal and local Russian leaders to visit the United States and observe its government and society.

Established at the Library of Congress as the Center for Russian Leadership Development in 2000, the center was renamed the Open World Leadership Center in 2003, when the program was

---

[22] P.L. 104-1, 109 Stat. 3, January 23, 1995. The act, as amended, applies 12 civil rights, labor, and workplace safety laws to Congress and certain legislative branch agencies. These laws are the Age Discrimination in Employment Act, Americans with Disabilities Act, Title VII of the Civil Rights Act of 1964, Employee Polygraph Protection Act, Fair Labor Standards Act, Family and Medical Leave Act, Federal Services Labor-Management Relations Act, Occupational Safety and Health Act of 1970, Rehabilitation Act of 1970, Veterans' employment and reemployment rights at Chapter 43 of Title 38 of the *U.S. Code*, Worker Adjustment and Retraining Act, and Veterans Employment Opportunities Act.

[23] Among the office's activities are administration of a dispute resolution process, investigation and enforcement of occupational safety and health and disability provisions of the act, investigation of labor relations and enforcement of applicable provisions, and development of educational programs regarding the act's provisions.

expanded to include specified additional countries.[24] In 2004, Congress further extended the program's eligibility to other countries designated by the center's board of trustees, subject to congressional consideration.[25] The center is housed in the Library and receives services from the Library through an inter-agency agreement.

The House-reported bill would provide $1.0 million, a decrease of $9.0 million (-90.0%), from the $10.0 million provided in FY2012 and requested for FY2013. The House report states that this funding level would "cover the cost associated with the shutdown" and directed "the program termination is to be finalized within one year of enactment of the Legislative Branch fiscal year 2013 appropriations bill."[26] The FY2012 level was $1.38 million (-12.1%) less than the $11.38 million provided in FY2011 (P.L. 112-10).

The FY2011 level represented a decrease of $623,000 (-5.2%) from the $12.00 million provided for FY2010, and the FY2010 level represented a decrease of $1.90 million (-13.7%) from the $13.90 million provided in the FY2009 Omnibus. The FY2009 level was a $4.92 million increase (54.8%) over the $8.98 million provided in FY2008, which was a decrease of $4.88 million (-35.2%) from the $13.86 million provided in FY2007 and FY2006.

Ongoing Discussion of Location of Open World

The location and future of Open World, as well as its inclusion in the legislative branch budget, have been a topic of discussion at appropriations hearings in recent fiscal years.

At the Senate FY2013 budget request hearing on March 1, 2012, the subcommittee discussed potential options for increasing private funding, including the hire of a development professional.

Previously, the House-passed FY2012 bill (H.R. 2551) would have provided $1.0 million, a decrease of 91.2% from the FY2011 level of $11.38 million. The House report stated, "The program has some strong champions on the Committee, but with reductions being made to most every program within the Federal budget the Committee has elected to shut down the program and recommends $1,000,000 for shutdown expenses."[27] The Senate-reported bill, in contrast, would have provided $10.0 million (-12.1% below the FY2011 level). The Senate report stated that "despite the fiscal constraints of the budget this program is necessary for the promotion of democratic principles in countries with historically oppressive rule."[28] The Consolidated Appropriations Act provides the Senate-reported level of $10.0 million.

---

[24] P.L. 106-554, 114 Stat. 2763, 2763A-120, December 21, 2000; P.L. 108-7, 117 Stat. 382, February 20, 2003. According to the 2003 act, the additional countries include "any country specified in §3 of the FREEDOM Support Act (22 U.S.C. 5801)," and "Estonia, Latvia, and Lithuania." The countries specified in 22 U.S.C. 5801 are Armenia, Azerbaijan, Belarus, Georgia, Kazakhstan, Kyrgyzstan, Moldova, Russia, Tajikistan, Turkmenistan, Ukraine, and Uzbekistan.

[25] P.L. 108-447, 118 Stat. 3192, December 8, 2004.

[26] U.S. Congress, House Committee on Appropriations, *FY2013 Legislative Branch Appropriations Bill*, H.Rept. 112-511, report to accompany H.R. 5882 (Washington: GPO, 2012), p. 42.

[27] U.S. Congress, House Appropriations Committee, *FY2012 Legislative Branch Appropriations Bill*, report to accompany H.R. 2551, H.Rept. 112-148 (Washington: GPO, 2011), p. 28.

[28] U.S. Congress, Senate Appropriations Committee, *FY2012 Legislative Branch Appropriations Bill*, report to accompany H.R. 2551, S.Rept. 112-80 (Washington: GPO, 2011), p. 45.

Additionally, the FY2010 House Appropriations Committee report stated that "the Legislative Branch Subcommittee has been clear that it expects the Open World program to become financially independent of funding in this bill as soon as possible."[29] This sentiment was also expressed in the conference report, which stated,

> The conferees are fully supportive of expanded efforts of the Open World Center to raise private funding and expect this effort to reduce the requirements for funding from the Legislative Branch appropriations bill in future years. The Committees look forward to a report of progress being made by the Center's fundraising program prior to hearings on its fiscal year 2011 budget request.[30]

The location within the legislative branch was discussed during a hearing on the FY2009 budget. Ambassador John O'Keefe, the executive director of Open World, testified that the program may attract different participants if associated with the executive branch rather than the Library of Congress, which may be seen as more neutral and nonpartisan.[31] The FY2009 explanatory statement directed the Open World Leadership Center Board of Trustees to work with the State Department and the judiciary to establish a shared funding mechanism.[32]

The subcommittees also had discussed this issue during the FY2008 appropriations cycle,[33] and language was included in the FY2008 Consolidated Appropriations Act requiring Open World to prepare a report by March 31, 2008, on "potential options for transfer of the Open World Leadership Center to a department or agency in the executive branch, establishment of the Center as an independent agency in the executive branch, or other appropriate options."[34] In 2004, GAO issued a report on the Open World program, examining program participation, purpose, and accountability.[35]

John C. Stennis Center for Public Service Training and Development

The center was created by Congress in 1988 to encourage public service by congressional staff through training and development programs.[36] The House-reported bill would not provide funding for the Stennis Center. The House report also states:

---

[29] U.S. House of Representatives, Committee on Appropriations, *Legislative Branch Appropriations Bill, 2010*, H.Rept. 111-160, (Washington: GPO, 2009), p. 29.

[30] U.S. Congress, *Legislative Branch Appropriations, 2010*, H.Rept. 111-265, conference report to accompany H.R. 2918 (Washington: GPO, 2009), p. 42.

[31] Testimony of Ambassador John O'Keefe, executive director, U.S. Congress, House Committee on Appropriations, Subcommittee on the Legislative Branch, *Legislative Branch Appropriations for 2009*, hearings, 110th Cong., 2nd sess., March 12, 2008 (Washington: GPO, 2008), pp. 359-420.

[32] *Congressional Record*, February 23, 2009, p. H2398.

[33] In H.R. 2771 (110th Cong.), the House-passed version of the FY2008 appropriations bill, the House Appropriations Committee recommended $6.0 million for Open World. The committee report stated that an additional $6.0 million would be provided for transfer to the program in the FY2008 State, Foreign Operations, and Related Programs appropriation. The House-passed bill, which retained the committee-recommended funding level, also contained an administrative provision transferring the Open World Leadership Center to the Department of State effective October 1, 2008. The Senate-reported bill (S. 1686, 110th Cong.) would have provided $13.5 million in new budget authority for Open World.

[34] P.L. 110-161, 121 Stat. 2251, December 26, 2007.

[35] Available at http://gao.gov/assets/250/241737.pdf.

[36] 2 U.S.C. 1105. See also http://www.stennis.gov/.

The fiscal year 2012 Conference Agreement (House Report 112–331) directed that future budget requests from the John C. Stennis Center be accompanied by an appropriately detailed budget justification as requested in House Report 112–148. The Committee did not receive such justification and therefore has not provided the requested funding.[37]

The Stennis Center had requested $430,000, the same level provided in FY2012. Previously, P.L. 112-10 provided $429,140 for FY2011 (including the 0.2% rescission), and $430,000 was provided in FY2010 and FY2009.

The following tables provide additional information on the FY2012 enacted and FY2013 requested levels for the legislative branch overall, the Senate, the House of Representatives, the Capitol Police, and the Architect of the Capitol.

Table 4. Legislative Branch Appropriations

(in thousands of dollars)

Entity	FY2012 Enacted	FY2013 Request	House Reported	Senate Reported	Enacted
Title I: Legislative Branch Appropriations					
Senate	868,592	910,515	—a		
House of Representatives	1,225,680	1,225,681	1,225,681		
Joint Items[b]	20,207	19,023	19,037		
Capitol Police[c]	340,137	373,769	360,137		
Office of Compliance	3,817	4,206	3,817		
Congressional Budget Office	43,787	44,637	44,280		
Architect of the Capitol	567,509	668,188	444,021a		
Library of Congress, Including CRS	587,344	603,589	592,642		
Congressional Research Service, Lib. of Cong.	*106,790*	*109,205*	*107,668*		
Government Printing Office	126,200	126,200	122,456		
Government Accountability Office	511,296	526,233	519,802		
Open World Leadership Center[d]	10,000	10,000	1,000		
Stennis Center for Public Service	430	430	0		
Title II: General Provisions	0	0	0		
Subtotal Legislative Branch (Titles I and II)	**4,304,999**	**4,512,471**	**3,332,873**		
CBO Scorekeeping Adjustment	2,000	0	0		
Total Legislative Branch (Titles I and II)	**4,306,999**	**4,512,471**	**3,332,873**		

Source: H.Rept. 112-331, H.Rept. 112-511, and the *FY2013 U.S. Budget.*

Notes:

a. By tradition, the House does not consider appropriations for internal Senate operations or Senate Office Buildings.

[37] U.S. Congress, House Committee on Appropriations, *FY2013 Legislative Branch Appropriations Bill*, H.Rept. 112-511, report to accompany H.R. 5882 (Washington: GPO, 2012), p. 20.

b. The FY2013 budget request contains the following under "Joint Items": the Joint Economic Committee, the Joint Committee on Taxation, the Office of the Attending Physician, and the Office of Congressional Accessibility Services. The FY2012 enacted level includes these items as well as $1.237 million for the Joint Congressional Committee on Inaugural Ceremonies of 2013.

c. This account was effective with the FY2003 Legislative Branch Appropriation Act. Previously, Capitol Police funds were contained under the joint items account.

d. The center was named the Center for Russian Leadership Development prior to FY2004. Appropriations represent payments to the center's trust fund.

Table 5. Senate Appropriations

(in thousands of dollars)

Accounts	FY2012 Enacted	FY2013 Request	Senate Reported	Enacted
Payments—Heirs of Deceased Members of Congress	0	0		
Expense Allowances and Representation	205	205		
Salaries, Officers, and Employees	175,762	182,067		
Office of Legislative Counsel	6,995	7,022		
Office of Legal Counsel	1,449	1,455		
Expense Allowances for Secretary of Senate, et al.	28	28		
Contingent Expenses (subtotal)	684,153	719,738		
Inquiries and Investigations	131,306	138,000		
Senate Intl. Narcotics Caucus	488	520		
Secretary of the Senate[a]	5,816	5,816		
Sergeant at Arms/Doorkeeper[b]	130,722	130,173		
Miscellaneous Items	19,360	19,360		
Senators' Official Personnel and Office Expense Account	396,180	425,569		
Official Mail Costs	281	300		
Total, Senate	**868,592**	**910,515**		

Source: H.Rept. 112-331 and the *FY2013 U.S. Budget.*

Notes:

a. Office operations of the Office of the Secretary of the Senate are also funded under "Salaries, Officers, and Employees."

b. Office operations of the Office of Sergeant at Arms and Doorkeeper are also funded under "Salaries, Officers, and Employees."

Table 6. House of Representatives Appropriations

(in thousands of dollars)

Accounts	FY2012 Enacted	FY2013 Request	House Reported	Enacted
Salaries and Expenses, Total	1,225,680	1,225,681	1,225,681	
House Leadership Offices	23,277	23,277	23,277	
House Leadership Offices (transition quarter)	5,818	—	—	
Members' Representational Allowance	573,939	573,939	573,939	
Committee Employees (subtotal)	152,631	153,031	152,631	
Standing Committees, Special and Select, except Appropriations	125,965	126,365	125,965	
Appropriations Committee	26,666	26,666	26,666	
Salaries, Officers, and Employees (subtotal)	177,628	174,912	173,669	
Office of the Clerk	26,114	22,370	22,370	
Office of the Sergeant at Arms	12,585	13,828	12,585	
Office of Chief Administrative Officer	116,782	116,782	116,782	
Office of Inspector General	5,045	4,692	4,692	
Office of General Counsel	1,415	1,415	1,415	
Office of the Chaplain	179	179	179	
Office of the Parliamentarian	2,060	2,060	2,060	
Office of the Law Revision Counsel	3,258	3,258	3,258	
Office of the Legislative Counsel	8,814	8,814	8,814	
Office of Interparliamentary Affairs	859	859	859	
Other Authorized Employees	347	485	485	
Office of Historian	170	170	170	
Allowances and Expenses (subtotal)	292,387	300,522	302,165	
Supplies, Materials, Administrative Costs and Federal Tort Claims	3,696	3,696	3,696	
Official Mail for committees, leadership, administrative and legislative offices	201	201	201	
Government Contributions	264,848	270,905	272,548	
Business Continuity and Disaster Recovery Emergency Appropriations	17,112	17,112	17,112	
Miscellaneous Items	760	760	760	
Transition Activities	1,722	4,125	4,125	
Wounded Warrior Program	2,500	2,175	2,175	
Office of Congressional Ethics	1,548	1,548	1,548	
House of Representatives, Total	**1,225,680**	**1,225,681**	**1,225,681**	

Sources: H.Rept. 112-331, H.Rept. 112-511, and the *FY2013 U.S. Budget.*

Table 7. Capitol Police Appropriations

(in thousands of dollars)

Accounts	FY2012 Enacted	FY2013 Request	House Reported	Senate Reported	Enacted
Salaries, Capitol Police	277,133	303,132	297,133		
General Expenses	63,004	70,637	63,004		
Total, Capitol Police	**340,137**	**373,769**	**360,137**		

Source: H.Rept. 112-331, H.Rept. 112-511, and the *FY2013 U.S. Budget.*

Table 8. Architect of the Capitol Appropriations

(in thousands of dollars)

Accounts	FY2012 Enacted	FY2013 Request	House Reported	Senate Reported	Enacted
General administration	101,340	102,601	90,755		
Capitol building	36,154	97,072	28,591		
Capitol grounds	9,852	18,502	17,152		
Senate office buildings	71,128	79,392	—a		
House of Representatives					
House office buildings	94,154	83,964	83,964		
House Historic Buildings Revitalization Fund	30,000	50,000	30,000		
Capitol power plantᵇ	123,229	118,533	108,616		
Library buildings and grounds	46,876	53,594	30,660		
Capitol Police buildings and grounds	21,500	30,802	20,867		
Botanic garden	12,000	12,140	12,140		
Capitol Visitor Center	21,276	21,588	21,276		
Total, Architect of the Capitol	**567,509**	**668,188**	**444,021**		

Source: H.Rept. 112-331, H.Rept. 112-511, and the *FY2013 U.S. Budget.*

Note:

a. The House does not consider appropriations for Senate office buildings.

b. Not including offsetting collections.

Appendix. Prior Fiscal Year Information and Resources

Table A-1. Overview of Legislative Branch Appropriations: FY1996-FY2012

House, Senate, Conference, and CRS Reports and Related Legislative Vehicles

Fiscal Year	House	Senate	Conference	Enacted	Enactment Vehicle Title	CRS Report
2012	H.Rept. 112-148 (H.R. 2551)	S.Rept. 112-80 (H.R. 2551)	H.Rept. 112-331 (H.R. 2055)	12/23/2011 (P.L. 112-74)	Consolidated Appropriations Act, 2012	CRS Report R41870, Legislative Branch: FY2012 Appropriations
2011	—	S.Rept. 111-294 (S. 3799)		4/15/2011 (P.L. 112-10)	Department of Defense and Full-Year Continuing Appropriations Act, 2011	CRS Report R41214, Legislative Branch: FY2011 Appropriations
2010	H.Rept. 111-160 (H.R. 2918)	S.Rept. 111-29 (S. 1294)	H.Rept. 111-265 (H.R. 2918)	10/1/2009 (P.L. 111-68)	Legislative Branch Appropriations Act, 2010	CRS Report R40617, Legislative Branch: FY2010 Appropriations
2009	—	—	explanatory materials inserted into the Congressional Record and issued in a committee print (H.R.1105)	3/11/2009 (P.L. 111-8)	Omnibus Appropriations Act, 2009	CRS Report RL34490, Legislative Branch: FY2009 Appropriations
2008	H.Rept. 110-198 (H.R. 2771)	S.Rept. 110-89 (S. 1686)	explanatory materials inserted into the Congressional Record (H.R. 2764)	12/26/2007 (P.L. 110-161)	Consolidated Appropriations Act, 2008	CRS Report RL34031, Legislative Branch: FY2008 Appropriations
2007	H.Rept. 109-485 (H.R. 5521)	S.Rept. 109-267 (H.R. 5521)	—	2/15/2007 (P.L. 110-5)	Revised Continuing Appropriations Resolution, 2007	CRS Report RL33379, Legislative Branch: FY2007 Appropriations
2006	H.Rept. 109-139 (H.R. 2985)	S.Rept. 109-89 (H.R. 2985)	H.Rept. 109-189 (H.R. 2985)	8/02/2005 (P.L. 109-55)	FY2006 Legislative Branch Appropriations Act	CRS Report RL32819, Legislative Branch: FY2006 Appropriations
2005	H.Rept. 108-577 (H.R. 4755)	S.Rept. 108-307 (S. 2666)	H.Rept. 108-792 H.R. 4818	12/8/2004 (P.L. 108-447)	Consolidated Appropriations Act, 2005	CRS Report RL32312, Appropriations for FY2005: Legislative Branch

Legislative Branch: FY2013 Appropriations

Fiscal Year	House	Senate	Conference	Enacted	Enactment Vehicle Title	CRS Report
2004	H.Rept. 108-186 (H.R. 2657)	S.Rept. 108-88 (S. 1383)	H.Rept. 108-279 (H.R. 2657)	9/30/2003 (P.L. 108-83)	Legislative Branch Appropriations Act, 2004	CRS Report RL31812, *Appropriations for FY2004: Legislative Branch*
2003	H.Rept. 107-576 (H.R. 5121)	S.Rept. 107-209 (S. 2720)	—	2/20/2003 (P.L. 108-7)	Consolidated Appropriations Resolution, 2003	CRS Report RL31312, *Appropriations for FY2003: Legislative Branch*
2002	H.Rept. 107-169 (H.R. 2647)	S.Rept. 107-37 (S. 1172)	H.Rept. 107-259 (H.R. 2647)	11/12/2001 (P.L. 107-68)	Legislative Branch Appropriations Act, 2002	CRS Report RL31012, *Appropriations for FY2002: Legislative Branch*
2001	H.Rept. 106-635 (H.R. 4516)	S.Rept. 106-304 (S. 2603)	H.Rept. 106-796 (H.R. 4516, incorporated into H.R. 4577)	12/21/2000 (P.L. 106-554)	Consolidated Appropriations Act, 2001	CRS Report RL30512, *Appropriations for FY2001: Legislative Branch*
2000	H.Rept. 106-156 (H.R. 1905)	S.Rept. 106-75 (S. 1206)	H.Rept. 106-290 (H.R. 1905)	9/29/1999 (P.L. 106-57)	Legislative Branch Appropriations Act, 2000	CRS Report RL30212, *Appropriations for FY2000: Legislative Branch*
1999	H.Rept. 105-595 (H.R. 4112)	S.Rept. 105-204 (S. 2137)	H.Rept. 105-734 (H.R. 4112)	10/21/1998 (P.L. 105-275)	Legislative Branch Appropriations Act, 1999	CRS Report 98-212, *Appropriations for FY1999: Legislative Branch*
1998	H.Rept. 105-196 (H.R. 2209)	S.Rept. 105-47 (S. 1019)	H.Rept. 105-254 (H.R. 2209)	10/7/1997 (P.L. 105-55)	Legislative Branch Appropriations Act, 1998	CRS Report 97-212, *Appropriations for FY1998: Legislative Branch*

Source: Congressional Research Service.

Selected Websites

These sites contain information on the FY2013 legislative branch appropriations requests and legislation, and the appropriations process:

House Committee on Appropriations
http://appropriations.house.gov/

Senate Committee on Appropriations
http://appropriations.senate.gov/

CRS Appropriations Products Guide
http://www.crs.gov/Pages/AppropriationsStatusTable.aspx?source=QuickLinks

Congressional Budget Office
http://www.cbo.gov

Government Accountability Office
http://www.gao.gov

Office of Management & Budget
http://www.whitehouse.gov/omb/

Author Contact Information

Ida A. Brudnick
Specialist on the Congress
ibrudnick@crs.loc.gov, 7-6460